C
O

Kirkby Stephen to Penrith

A fabulous 42-mile heritage trail through the
Eden, Lyvennet & Lowther valleys

Mark Richards

First published in 2017 by
PathMaster
An imprint of J R Nicholls
Denby Dale HD8 8RT

Text, photographs & illustrations © Mark Richards 2017

All rights reserved. No part of this book may be reproduced or utilised in any form or by any means, electronic or mechanical, including photocopying, or by any information storage and retrieval system, without permission in writing from the publisher.

The rights of Mark Richards to be identified as the author of this work have been asserted by him in accordance with the Copyright, Designs and Patents Act 1988.

ISBN: 978-1-911347-52-1

Printed and bound in Great Britain by
CPI Group (UK) Ltd, Croydon CR0 4YY

Disclaimer: Whilst every care and effort has been taken in the preparation of this book, the reader should be aware that walking can be a dangerous activity and conditions can be variable. Therefore, neither J R Nicholls Publishing nor the Author accept liability for damage of any nature (including damage to property, personal injury or death) arising directly or indirectly from the information in this book.

The Countryside Code

Be safe - plan ahead and follow any signs

Leave gates and property as you find them

Protect plants and animals, and take your litter home

Keep dogs under close control

Consider other people

CASTLES of EDEN WALK
67km / 42 miles

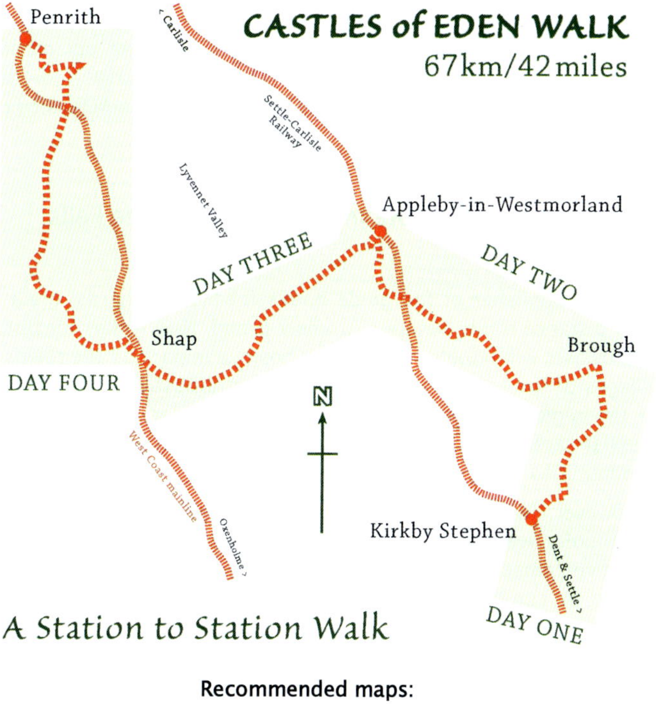

Penrith

Carlisle

Settle-Carlisle Railway

Lyvennet Valley

Appleby-in-Westmorland

DAY THREE

DAY TWO

Shap

Brough

DAY FOUR

West Coast mainline

Oxenholme

Kirkby Stephen

Dent & Settle

DAY ONE

A Station to Station Walk

Recommended maps:

Kirkby Stephen to Maulds Meaburn (page 26)
Ordnance Survey Explorer Series   OL19

Shap to Penrith
Ordnance Survey Explorer Series   OL5

Fix the Fells is a collaborative partnership programme between the National Trust, the Lake District National Park, Nurture Lakeland, Friends of the Lake District, Natural England and Cumbria County Council. The aim of the Fix the Fells partnership is to protect the spectacular Lakeland fells from erosion and damage by repairing and maintaining the upland paths of the Lake District. For more information, visit fixthefells.co.uk.

Publisher's note in support of Fix the Fells

As the publisher of the guide books for Mark Richards' great new long distance trails, we are extremely proud. New routes for outdoor enthusiasts will hopefully provide a positive impact on the towns and villages of the Lake District, taking the enthusiastic walker into parts of the region not usually on the tourist trail, as well as the more familiar areas. We hope this has a beneficial impact on the communities alongside these routes.

However, whilst there is hopefully a positive impact to the community we are keenly aware that there is the potential for a negative impact on the very fells and footpaths that facilitate the routes. A combination of millions of pairs of walking boots, the weather and gradient means erosion is a constant problem. To this end, we have committed to donating a proportion of the revenue from the sale of each guide to 'Fix the Fells'.

We are very proud to support their work. If you would like to find out more, and maybe give a donation of your own or even volunteer to help, you can find further details about their work at www.fixthefells.co.uk.

We hope you enjoy these new guides.

DEDICATION

To Simon and Wendy Bennett of Augill Castle Hotel

For championing the highest standards of hospitality in the Eden valley, as too their broader contribution to the Cumbrian tourism industry and international perspective, exemplified by www.bridgesnotbarriers.com.

ACKNOWLEDGEMENTS

I could never disguise my adoration of Eden, a cherished land of green rolling hills and sequestered vales set between the mountains of Lakeland and the high Pennine moors. I am far from alone and I would be failing in my duty if I did not take this opportunity to mention at least some of those who live and work at its heart, sustaining a welcome to visitors and sense of community. Perhaps best exemplifying the latter spirit, Rev Sarah Lunn of Long Marton. Others in this mould are councillors Joan Johnstone and Alex Birtles from Kirkby Stephen Town Council; Stan Rooke, Deputy Mayor of Appleby; Scott Jackson, Deputy Mayor of Penrith and Karen Greenwood of Kirkby Thore. In addition to these, artist Ann Sandell, national secretary of Walkers are Welcome, from Kirkby Stephen, Pat Jones from Swanson House in Brough, Andy Connell in Appleby and, of course, not forgetting the commitment of the Eden District Tourism team: Jessica Goodfellow, Sally Hemsley and Charlie Thornton. Honestly, the list of ambassadors is longer than I have scope to express here. As a final personal note of admiration the lamented East Cumbria Countryside Project left a remarkable legacy of Discover Eden trails, round rambles marked by post-mounted plaques reflecting the richness of the area's rural heritage. Several are encountered on this walk and they are a worthy quest in themselves, created from the exquisite linocuts of Pip Hall (www.piphall.co.uk).

Foreword

I am thrilled and delighted to recommend to you this outstanding walk through the beautiful Eden valley. There are many printed walks available in many areas of England. Why should you choose this one? Let me give you some clues:

·   The peacefulness and beauty of the Valley – You will be traversing two National Parks which include areas of Special Scientific Interest and of nationally important wildlife reserves. The River Eden is a jewel to behold at any time of the year.

The wildlife in the Valley is amazing- we have Red Squirrels (and no Greys) and a paradise for bird watchers.

·   "This is a landscape brimming with history" writes Mark and he is right. – you will pass through three town centre Conservation Areas and potentially visit castles at Pendragon, Brough, Appleby, Brougham, Lowther and Penrith. Along the way are old and ancient houses, barns and interesting vernacular buildings. You will not be bored!

Mark often touches on the meanings of place-names in medieval Old English, Norse, and old dialect words. He explains how the names are reflected in the places and it brings the walk alive!

·   The Eden Valley is in the rain shadow of the Lake District National Park You can have all the beauty of the Eden valley and far less of the rain!

- The quality of the welcome and the hospitality - we pride ourselves on being a friendly and welcoming place with outstanding locally produced food and drink. If you want more information please contact one of our excellent award winning Tourist Information Centres.

I hope you enjoy this walk and come back to Eden again and again! Good luck.

Karen Greenwood

Senior Tourist Information Assistant, Appleby

2017

CASTLES
OF
EDEN

CASTLES of EDEN WALK
A Journey Through Time

Kirkby Stephen to Penrith   67km/42miles

Kirkby Stephen station lies on England's most scenic railway journey, the Settle-Carlisle. You may travel from Leeds, off the East Coast mainline, or Lancaster and Carlisle, from the West Coast mainline. Mindful that the first walking stage to Church Brough is only an easy-going four-hour saunter you might opt to include that in your day's travel. Though more likely you will be happy to complete your initial train journey and stay locally.

Kirkby Stephen railway station

With the use of taxis from the outset you may stay in Kirkby Stephen, Brough or Appleby or nearby village accommodation in-between. It is quite practical to consider staying two or three nights in the one place, forward and back tracking in the taxi. Though with a little aforethought and advance booking you can one-night stand at the end of each walking day.

Treasure in Waiting

A procession of field-paths in an undulating landscape, the very essence of the English country idyll. However, boots are pre-requisite footwear, with rain gaiters an asset too. There are no great gradients nor hills to climb, just the pleasantest of country walking throughout. The route takes in some lovely villages, especially meritorious Maulds Meaburn, Crosby Ravensworth, Bampton and Askham. The first two days are guided by the Eden, while day three leads cross-country via the Lyvennet valley and the final day sweeps down the Lowther to the Eamont. All amid scenery of the highest order, on a route uniquely pioneered for Northern Rail travellers' delight.

Keeping pace with history, station to station

This is a landscape brimming with history, at every turn the Eden Castles Walk throws up clues to the past. Ancient stones, earthworks, field boundaries and ruins dot the countryside tantalising the enquiring mind, even the towns and villages beg questions to fascinate and intrigue. Both Norman castles at Brough and Brougham rest on the outline earthworks of Roman forts. The very presence of castles from many ages affirm a region beset with ancient challenge and potential conflict - the Warcop military firing range reflecting a contemporary national need to be prepared.

For walkers eager to make more of the expedition the walk can include a longer opening sequence lassoing the enigmatic Pendragon Castle, located at the dramatic Pennine entry to Mallerstang, where the Eden is born. Thereafter, heading downstream by the ruined Lammerside pele and defended manor of Wharton Hall to link up with the direct route at Halfpenny House, thereby almost doubling the first day's trek.

The Walk concludes in close proximity to the Far Eastern Fells of Lakeland drawing down the Lowther to pass the fantasy castle associated with the Earls of Lonsdale, passing through Clifton where the last land battle on English soil occurred in 1745 when the Duke of Cumberland's red-coat militia confronted the retreating army of Bonnie Prince Charlie. Once over the Eamont the route concludes in chime with a Roman road to end in Penrith, the administrative heart of the Eden District, where you may board your train or bus connection home.

ROUTE GUIDE

DAY 1:   Kirkby Stephen to Church Brough
DAY 2:   Church Brough to Appleby-in-Westmorland
DAY 3:   Appleby-in-Westmorland to Shap
DAY 4:   Shap to Penrith
FINISH: Customising Your Station to Station Walk

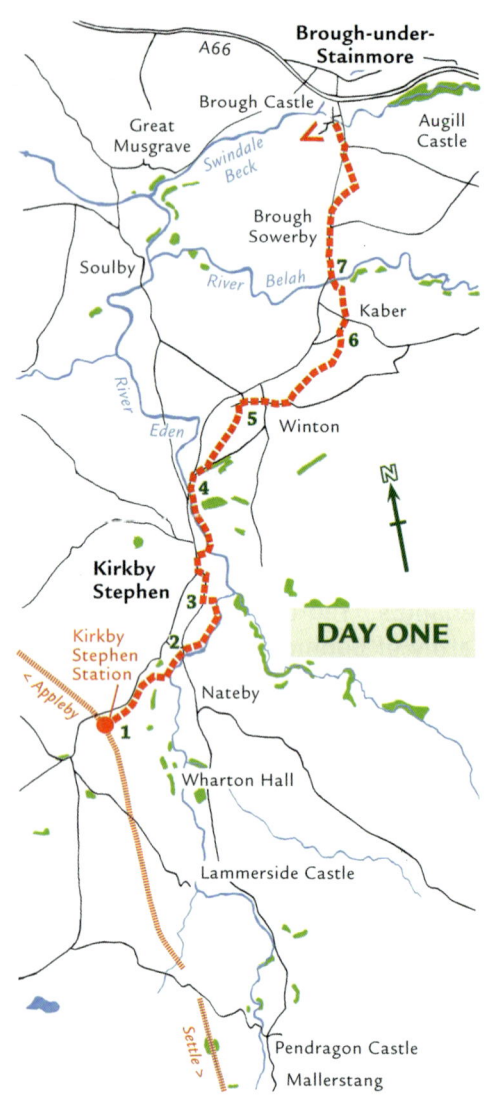

DAY ONE   Kirkby Stephen Station to Church Brough
11km | 7 miles   4 hours

Stand on the footbridge spanning the railway track at Kirkby Stephen station and take a moment to sense the remarkable landscape setting. This is rural Britain at its most compelling, a wonderful sweeping panorama of green pastures and backing mountains, utterly beautiful to behold - instantly you have itchy feet. Your first day's hike on the Castles of Eden Walk sets its sights on Brough Castle little more than seven miles distant. A gentle rambling journey that quickly connects with the youthful River Eden, visits the little town of Kirkby Stephen and then traverses pastures via the shy Westmorland villages of Winton, Kaber and Brough Sowerby.

1 Exit the station following the blue walking man/cycle sign guiding through the car park and down the approach road a little way to a gate accessing the Station Walk. This tarmac path leads downhill beside a drystone wall - this was once seven feet high bounding the C16th Wharton deer park - the path a tremendous recent creation linking the station and town most pleasantly. En route you may notice the second World War pill box on the adjacent pasture bank of Whinny Hill - not an allusion to horses rather a lost growth of gorse - and hard right as you look towards Mallerstang Edge the high source of the Eden, a hill terraced with lynchets. These cultivation strips of medieval origin are associated with the lost village of Wharton.

The path sweeps through a hollow and, rising, passes through a gate arriving at Halfpenny House - originally a beer-house, serving a tankard of ale at a most appetising price! The sign encourages cyclists to turn left for the town. But the attractive option for walkers is straight on via the field-gate advancing beside the tall drystone wall to a fence-stile and immediately left wall-stile, overlooking a steep wooded bank of the River Eden. After the next wall-end stile the path declines with the pasture, to witness the river's confining entry into limestone bedrock. Coming to a flight of private steps veer right down the path steps, skirting under the buttress of an old railway bridge to come back up steps and along the narrow path beside a wall within the thunderous gorge. Further steps lead to a hand-gate onto the Nateby road.

2 Turn left and enter Stenkrith Park at the kissing-gate on the right. You may keep with the upper path to peer through the road-bridge arch at the gorge from the cast-iron footbridge. But you do need to descend into the gorge left, so don't cross the bridge. The earlier path descends on a gentler course coming into the open woodland carpeted with wild garlic (during late spring) close to the rock-bed threading river and the first of several attractive stones featuring poetic inscriptions about the Eden and its environs, part of the two-mile long Poetry Path - its 12 stones depict the farming year in verse by Meg Peacocke, inscribed by Pip Hall, on either side of the river. The popular way leads on by a fence-stile into pasture coming to a kissing-gate. Keep riverside on the long meadow, passing the threesome

'December' stone motif to reach Swingy Bridge, no longer dubiously loose. The walk does not cross. Instead, slip through the walled kissing-gate – just inside the gate on the left is the January stone - and follow the charming confined lane to regain the Nateby road at Bollam Cottage B&B.

3 Follow the footway into town, the street bends left at the primary school coming by the chunky classical architecture of Temperance Hall, with its blue-frocked statue of Temperance. At the traffic lights enter the Market Street turning left, with diverse shopping choice and places of refreshment and night's repose. Two eye-catching elements are adapted chapels, one a youth hostel, the other The Emporium, a tempting delicatessen and post office. Further along the street you'll find the Upper Eden Visitor Centre, if open a useful port of call for local information pertinent to your Country Tracks time trekking. Next comes The Cloisters arcade entry to the churchyard. The parish church fully merits an admiring inspection, locally dubbed the Cathedral of the Dales. Many choose to seek out the Loki Stone inside, depicting the Norse God of Mischief bound in chains. The walk veers right in front of The Cloisters following the narrow Stoneshot alley to descend steps and cross Frank's Bridge spanning the Eden. Ignore the Coast to Coast Walk fingerpost, go straight ahead passing in front of the cricket pavilion. The parrot motif is a reminder of the occasional sighting one might get of this colourful bird now liberated and free-flying. The fenced ground keeps sheep and rabbits at bay. The riverside path seeks a

Upper Eden Visitor Centre in Kirkby Stephen

footbridge over Hartley Beck thereby joining Hartley Road. Keep forward to Lowmill Bridge at the entrance to the football ground. Leave the road, following the narrow riverside path - if the river is flowing strongly then cross the bridge and follow the matching path through the woodyard on the higher west bank. A little bridge and then a sharp rise brings the path up to the main road at a hand-gate beside New Bridge.

4 At this point the walk diverts from the Eden, the next time encountered it will be more substantial, following the transfusion of three considerable watercourses, Scandal, Swindale Becks and the River Belah. Go right with the roadside footway and after Eden Mount bear first right with Kirkbank Lane (by-road). After the entrance to Eden Place, where the macaws live, cross the fence-stile left and traverse the field half-right on the path signed 'Winton'. A fence-stile in an intermediate boundary leads to the corner of a second field and another fence-stile; keep forward to a stile in a tiny section of wall beside a gate. Head on to a fence-stile and cross the next field coming by a hedge corner passing under a power line to reach a stile in a short section of wall with attendant sheep creep. Bear half-left to find a stile and footbridge to the right of a Scots pine wood. After rain the next 100m can be damp, only partially alleviated by the flags. Rise up the field under a bower of beech to a narrow hand-gate in the corner following a wall-confined path to the street in Winton.

5 Turn right following the village street with its characterful mix of dwellings, including the attention grabbing three-storey Manor House of 1776, once a notorious Dickens-style boys' school. Come by the tiny green, where you'll spot the Millennium stone, set between the old school and the play area, with the Bay Horse Inn beyond. At the end of the village beneath Hilltop, come by Stonelea to a field-gate and twin-footpath sign. Bear half-right with the path signed 'Kaber', rounding a wall corner to stride the length of the long but comparatively narrow pasture field. Cross a fence-stile and continue to a further fence-stile from where you bear left to a hand-gate and plank bridge spanning Rookby Beck. Keep right, alongside the beck and continuing field hedge boundary, rounding a hedge bend. The field tapers to a gate/stile cross and keep forward with the left-hand hedge to a stile entering a short green lane to a gate beside a bungalow, stepping onto the minor road.

6 Go right to reach the Kaber road-sign backed by the 'Best Kept Hamlet in Eden' sign. Kaber translates as 'jackdaw hill'. You can admire the tranquil hamlet by following the road right - but backtrack to continue. Remarkably, Kaber has its place in history as a hot-bed of Parliamentary unrest with the failed English Civil War rising in 1663 against Charles II, known as the Kaber Rigg Plot. Cruelly, its leaders were hung at Appleby. The walk skips immediately left before the community sign, via the metal field-gate footpath sign 'Belah Bridge'. Step over the stone slab spanning the ditch and follow the bank to the stile and footbridge over Popping Beck. Advance by the fence-stile left of the gate and follow the open track to avoid the damp rushy ground to bear half-left up the pasture bank venturing the length of the extended pasture to a fence-stile in the far corner. Skip across a short neck of land (at the time of research a crop of barley was growing) to a corresponding fence-stile and descend the bank onto the meadow naturally drawn left to a squeeze-stile beside a gate left of Belah Bridge.

7 Cross this retired road bridge and come onto the broad verge of the A685. A tangible grass path exists leading to the junction opposite the Belah Bridge Inn in Brough Sowerby. Pass over by the seat and follow on to join a track descending to a gate by a shed entering the meadow. Stride on to follow left the tall hedge which curves gently to a gateway and on to the prominent stone field-barn. Beyond, find a stile next to a bath trough. Immediately after, cross the stile left and rise with the hedge to the left to a fence-stile beside a clump of sycamore trees. Go forward through the open pasture bearing down to a wall-stile regaining the verge of the A685. Follow this to the minor road junction of Leacett Lane and a few yards beyond carefully cross the main road to slip through an access path into the old road. This former thoroughfare leads to the peaceful centre of Church Brough. If you have booked accommodation in Market Brough keep forward to follow the continuing footway under the A66 flyover.

Augill Castle Hotel

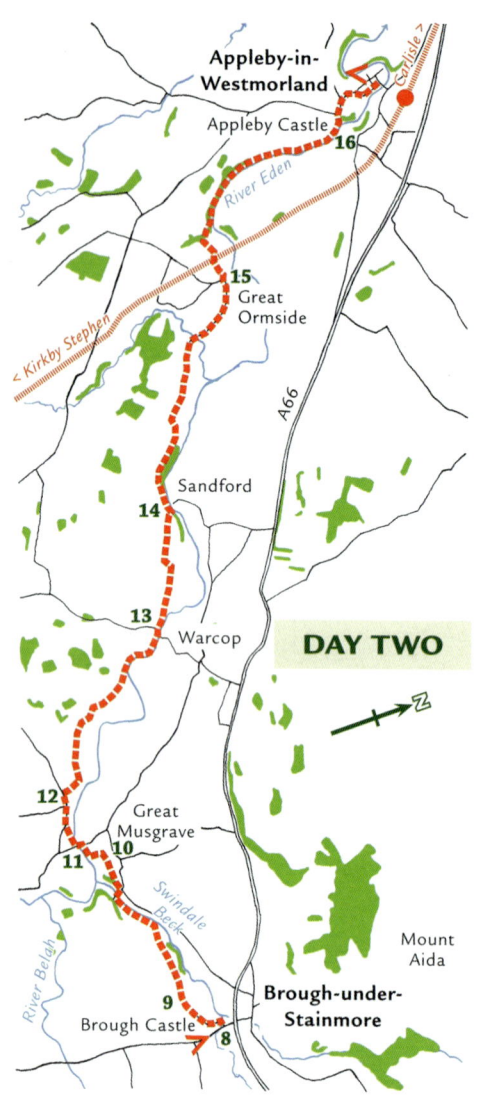

DAY TWO   Church Brough to Appleby-in-Westmorland
17km | 10 miles   6 hours

A second valley-questing day travelling with Swindale Beck to re-connect with the Eden at Great Musgrave. There is but one port of call for refreshment during this stage, being the pub at Sandford.

8 Turn left by the central parking area. Ahead find free access to Brough Castle (English Heritage) and perhaps no less appealing Brough Castle Farm's tempting ice cream parlour! Turn left down the narrow wiend (passageway), passing the entrance to St Michael's church. Like the castle, this is well worth close scrutiny. Long and low, its sturdy masonry culminates in a massive tower, best seen from the west. The fine mullion windows lend a pleasing grace to a classic Eden edifice. The continuing lane slips through a red sandstone cutting. Behind the house 'Manderley' stands the old vicarage, a considerable building in its own

Brough Castle

right. Fork right via the gate, rising up the track to a gate with an attractive bronze plate on a post with flowers and a military helicopter motif. To the right you get the best of all views of Brough Castle's impressive setting. Together with the faint outlines of the preceding Roman fort of Verterae, the first evidence of military defence in this area, both in their time commanded the important trans-Pennine trade route crossing from Stainmore. The rumbling sound of A66 lorries, overlaid during weekdays by the rhythmic chatter of machine guns and exploding mortars, give a hint of what it must be like to live in a war zone: the result of training activities on the MOD's Warcop ranges. For all that the air is charged with anger and rage, the walk succeeds in soothing the spirit as one drifts through a historically rich landscape, where farming and nature have worked hand-in-hand over countless generations.

9 Passing along the ridge-top hedge lane the route emerges at a gate bearing down to a small stone barn. Keep right to a hand-gate. Follow on gently down the slope to a further hand-gate and brief hollow-way into the meadow. Your attention will be arrested by the strip lynchets on the bank half-right: striking evidence of cultivation from medieval times. Advance to a metal hand-gate, with a second bronze plate, this time poignantly depicting a scene of feudal tillage. Advance with the fence coming beside Swindale Beck. Just as the beck is actively eroding the eastern bank of Brough Castle, so too is it taking giant bites off this meadow. So now the power-line has been defended by a metal barrier, further along willow has been used to far less durable effect and latterly stone blocks have been set into the near bank to contain the appetite of the surging waters. Find a third plate depicting oyster catchers, beyond the galvanized field-gate. Go right with the fenced lane, crossing the farm bridge to reach Hallgarth. Turn left and go through the first field-gate left, ascending the pasture bank. Beneath your feet is an ascending sequence of cultivation terraces, most impressive. Also absorb the magnificent view of the Pennine escarpment. Pass through an open hedge to reach a stile in a tiny section of wall. Pass by the cottage row to a metal hand-gate into a walled lane leading to the road in the midst of Great Musgrave, where the village-name of Saxon origin meant 'the mouse-infested ditch'. The word 'grave' exists in modern speech as the term for hard work ie. 'to graft', as in dig ditches!

Strip lynchets at Great Musgrave

10 Turn left guided by the bridleway sign directing to 'St Theobald's'. Quickly enter a hedge-confined tarmac path, latterly with a hand-rail, leading smartly down to the riverside church. Enter the Church Field at a gate. The adjacent renovated stone barn has a set of fascinating interpretative boards. So, to confirm the nearness of the Eden to the church, it had to be re-built in 1845 after a ruinous flood. The dedication is unusual, St Theobald being the patron saint of charcoal burners! Follow with the riverbank to a metal gate into the B6295 Warcop to Kirkby Stephen road. Go left to cross Musgrave Bridge.

11 Once across, find a footpath sign directing right. The path weaves through the lightly wooded area between a weir and the abutment of an old railway from Clifton Junction near Penrith to Kirkby Stephen, which operated for a century until 1962 – the Eden Valley Railway Society have aspirations to revive the line. From a kissing-gate, come up the bank to traverse the pasture parallel with the river and then go through another kissing-gate onto a small triangular open space leading to the Swillings Lane road in Little Musgrave. Keep forward, noting the old AA sign on the cottage wall at the junction if, for no other reason, than to know that you are 267½ miles from Hyde Park Corner in London - measured before the advent of motorways! Pass on by Little Musgrave Farm to leave the road right via the cattle-grid onto the concrete track for Ploughlands.

12 Follow this long farm access way into a hedged lane at a second cattle-grid, opening again at a further cattle

-grid. The open track swings left, approaching a farm (with holiday lets barn conversions) to approach Ploughlands Farm, first recorded as Plewlands in 1539. Find a stile/footbridge left leading onto a rough strip above the beck and beside a fence below the portal farm buildings. This leads to a fence-stile right from where ascend the pasture with the hedge close right to reach and cross a fence-stile at the top corner. Enter a green lane, well used by farm tractors. Duly this opens into a pasture and runs on with handsome views once more down to the River Eden, coming through to a gate and along a slightly sunken way with a fence close right well above the river on Bermer Scar (a curious name that translates as 'the marsh cleared by burning'). This drifts down to a metal wicket-gate proceeding now at river level and emerging into an open meadow, advancing along the riverbank to slip through a squeeze-stile in the wall connected to Warcop Bridge.

13 Warcop is renowned for its military training area where tanks and infantry pepper the Pennine fellside, going through their noisy paces. The Old Eden Valley Railway is operating trains on the restored line. You can visit on Sundays from Easter to September and on Bank Holidays, the rides are usually on the hour. Don't cross the bridge, as there is sadly no pub in the village. By contrast Sandford, the next village downstream, has retained a popular hostelry! So keep forward with the road and as this bears left keep ahead, guided by the 'Little Ormside' bridleway sign. The roadway rises and curves right. Find a further bridleway sign directing left with a lane well-used by farm tractors. As this veers left, keep on with the green lane, proceeding by the gate. Now something of a tunnel, the hedges are over-due laying. Emerging at a gate follow on with the open track with a fence close right, swing right on entry into the next field, leaving the track to go through the broken field-gate ahead. The path leads over the brow of a chunky set of strip lynchet terraces, with a big duck pond in view below draining Black Sike. You can see more lynchets on Sourlands Hill over to the left. The bridleway leads on north-west via a field-gate, shortly switching sides of the hedge at a bridle-gate to come down beside the fence to a hand-gate, close by a bungalow. Keep forward to come by a stile onto a summer-glorious wild flower margin beside the beck and turn right to reach a bridle-gate onto the roadway beside Sandford Bridge. If you relish a pub then cross the Eden, following Haregate road into the hamlet to visit the Sandford Arms, a welcome intermediate place of refreshment and cosy accommodation.

14 The Eden Castles Walk keeps to the west of the river following the access track to and through Blacksyke Farm, a busy Friesian dairy farm. Beyond the barns find a footpath sign 'Little Ormside' and gate to the right of a concrete block shed and feed tower. Ascend the slope with a hedge close left coming above Tricklebanks Wood to a hand-gate. Follow on beside the wood in the pasture, noting the curious dyke feature inside the wood close right. At a broken gate the wood is left behind and a continuing track draws the footpath downhill with fence left, opening at a gateway to run on unenclosed to a gate entering a green lane, well-used by tractors. Come by a newly cobbled ford and footbridge to reach and pass Terry's Farm at Little Ormside. After Ormside Lodge Farm, follow on with the road crossing Helm Beck to reach Great Ormside. The pub has gone. However, you should make the tiny detour right to view St James. Set on a prominent knoll well above the river the site must have ancient significance. The discovery of the Ormside Bowl in the churchyard in 1823 reinforces this view. Dating from the mid-C8th, it is one of the most treasured Anglo-Saxon artifacts in England (on display at York Museum) – it is thought the bowl was buried in later centuries having originally been in the church. In 1898 a Viking warrior burial was found including his sword. Ormside means 'the seat of Orm' a C10th Viking family who established the basis of what is now Ormside Hall below the church.

15 Head straight over following the farm lane signed 'Permissive Path Walkers Only'. This leads to a bridge underpass of the Settle-Carlisle Railway embankment coming to a gate/ladder-stile, where you enter the field. Head forward to bear left into a hedged pasture passage. At the end bear right, by-passing the redundant stile, slipping through a small hollow to a fence-stile where you will find a bronze motif on a post depicting quaint medieval creatures, the creative handiwork of Pip Hall. The narrow path can be awkward and muddy leading down to cross a footbridge spanning Jeremy Gill - spot the red squirrel feeder just downstream on the right. Ascend by a second bronze motif post, this time depicting an elegant iris design, besides a fence-stile. Cross and wander along the top of the coppice woodland, duly finding a flight of wooden retainer steps on an oft muddy path leading down to the Eden's banks. The path winds on through the wood by a plank bridge, latterly coming a little too near the water's edge. River erosion is a factor that may cause you to hug the left side of the path glad to reach a fence-stile exiting the wood into the meadow. March merrily on to slip through a copse via stiles to again stroll along the meadow beside the tree-lined Eden. The meadow way ends at a muddy stile where the path becomes confined, coming by a wall to a kissing-gate stepping onto the road.

16 Ignore the inviting footbridge right, the walk goes left rising beneath the high banks of Appleby Castle grounds, joining the footway beside the B6260 along Scattergate. A curious name that actually derives from the Old English word scitere meaning 'open sewer', quite the reverse of what you see today. Spot Doomgate bearing down left, this indicates a 'street where trials were held'. The footway swings round by Shaw's Wiend to reach the castle gates at the top of Boroughgate. Appleby Castle is open to the public during the summer season for guided tours and access to the grounds. The castle has a café and tavern and, throughout the year, there are special ticketed events such as open air performances of works by Shakespeare. There are also B&B facilities and holiday cottages in the Inner Bailey. More information can be found at the castle website, www.applebycastle.co.uk.

The castle was first mentioned in 1176, presumably when the Viponts built the first keep, with an inner and outer bailey. The great structure we see today known as Caesar's Tower was restored in 1651, the name is quite simply a fanciful invention. It is beautifully topped by turrets with pretty lanterns decoratively added in 1784.

The Cliffords took over the castle in the late C13th, later coming to the Earls of Thanet.

The High Cross carries a motto attributed to Lady Anne Clifford "Retain your Loyalty, preserve your Rights". Descend Boroughgate on the right-hand side, taking a little time to glance in at The Almshouses known as St Anne's Hospital (in the old sense of hospitality). Visitors are welcome to visit the little Chapel in the courtyard (donations in the box are welcome too!). No visit to Appleby is complete without a reflective and respectful admiration of this charming courtyard where local single ladies find a late life comfortable, if a trifle cramped, abode. The tree-lined hill is blessed with a succession of handsome houses, lower down

High Cross, Boroughgate, Appleby-in-Westmorland

some fascinating shops too. Passing on by the Tourist Information Centre in the Moot Hall and Tufton Arms by the Cross, you might enter the churchyard via the Cloisters added in 1810 by the Town Council who employed the architect Robert Smirke (who also designed London Buildings and Lowther Castle). Lady Anne Clifford is buried in St Lawrence's, very near to her Clifford Memorial and near to her mother Lady Margaret. St Lawrence's echoes of a former prosperous age and, like the castle, was rebuilt in part by Lady Anne, whose influence we will find again at Brougham.

Appleby, which means 'the farmstead with an apple orchard', became the head of the Barony and County of Westmorland. In 1974 with local government changes it was merged with Cumberland and Lancashire beyond Morecambe Bay to re-form Cumbria – the name has historic prescient having C10th Celtic origins, when all the country from the mouth of the Clyde to the Bay was deemed to be Cumbria "the land of our fellow people". Appleby remains a vibrant little town beautifully set upon a twist in the river and is synonymous with an annual Horse Fair, when gypsies and travellers descend upon the town in the first week of June, bringing colour and quirky life to the place.

Lady Anne's Hospital Almshouses

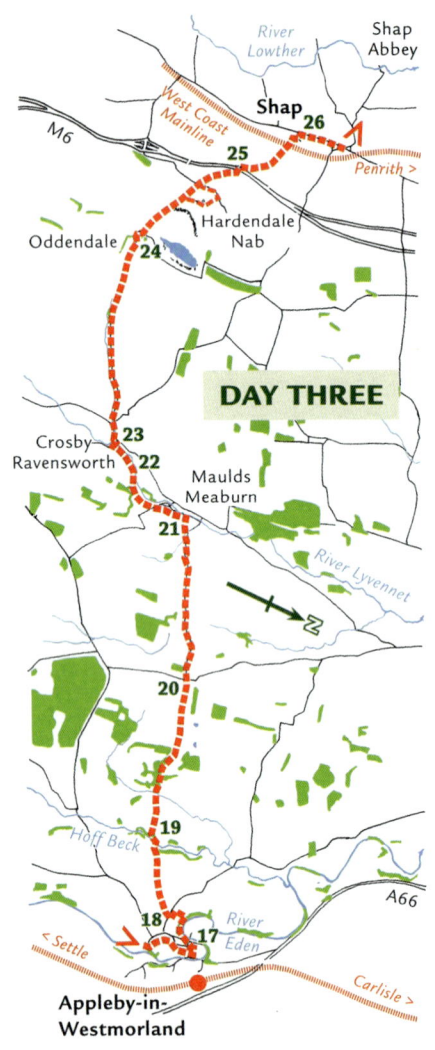

DAY THREE   Appleby-in-Westmorland to Shap
17km/10 miles   6 hours

Breaking from the Eden we cut across the grain of the landscape slicing through the delightful Lyvennet valley. Once again there is only one hostelry en route, the community-hub pub in Crosby Ravensworth, welcome inn indeed.

17 The route turns left along Low Wiend, bearing left with Chapel Street, at the end meeting Holme Street, slant half-right into the rising Banks Lane. Climbing, this becomes a footway part-way up. Cast your last view of the River Eden on the Castles of Eden Walk as it skirts Holme meadow, scene of Horse Fair trap races. The trap races are usually called Harness Racing and are to British Harness Racing standards. They are on May Bank Holiday (end of May), Horse Fair weekend, and August Bank Holiday. Watch, as the path reaches its highest point, for a branch left within a short panelled passage accessing Margaret Way. Turn left to reach the road where you bear left after 120m, seeking a green lane right bridleway sign 'Tollbar Cottage'.

18 Follow the green lane (which can be muddy) and, after a stream crosses the bridleway, the path enters an even narrower hedged lane leading to a hand-gate. Go diagonally across to the facing stile - thereby leaving the bridle-lane which here turns left en route to Tollbar Cottage. Entering the pasture field, follow the hedge on the right with a long view back to Appleby Castle backed by the High Cup valley and Murton Pike. Coming by a tin-boarded sheepfold, cross the fence-stile and head diagonally across the next field, crossing a plank in a ditch to reach the next fence-stile, beside a field-gate. Pass on by the shallow banks of a former field boundary to angle down the long slope left to a wall-stile. Coming adjacent to Rachel's Wood, take the fence-stile to arrive at and cross Bandley Bridge spanning Hoff Beck. The term 'hoff' is thought to allude to a heathen temple, associated with early Scandinavian settlement in the area.

19 Bear left in the meadow and slip through a kissing-gate into light woodland. Now a bridle-path, this is prone to be muddy although the duck-boarding helps. This ascends a hollow-way, you might find it easier on the left-hand side to reach the gate. A broad damp bridle-lane now ensues, leading ultimately to a field-gate keeping forward with the rough margin that leads down to a marshy patch before a hand-gate and stone-arched bridge spanning Nether Hoff Sike. Keep forward via a gate entering the open woodland of Big Clinch (curious name) where damp ground is unavoidable. Exit at a galvanized gate and soon go through the weak hand-gate/even frailer ladder-stile keeping with the marshy fringe of woodland to escape the dampness at a field-gate. Entering a pasture with a coppice woodland close left, march on, undulating up to a galvanized gate to enter a fenced lane. Maintain your south-westerly course now on a welcome firm track to reach a gate onto the Longrigg road at a 'T' junction. Note the neat trimmed beech hedges.

20 Walk straight ahead with Brackenslack Lane, signed 'Maulds Meaburn'. This road passes the entrance to several farms all with revealing names, most alluding to the underlying limestone: Dryevers 'summer dry stream'; Holesfoot 'pot-hole hollow'; Trainlands 'great crane frequented pasture' (this is a form of heron now only resident in small numbers in East Anglia, a handsome bird famed for its astonishing trumpeting call); Greyber 'limestone hill'; while Brackenslack itself means 'bracken-festooned dry stream'. Coming down the hill after Brackenslack Farm watch for a footpath sign 'Maulds Meaburn' on the left and a wall-stile over a gill. Head down, crossing the plank footbridge over Scattergate Gill - you'll remember what this name meant from Appleby, though again it's no long applicable. Traverse the field to a ladder-stile in the hedge corner. Bear right, soon descending the narrow horse-grazed field passing to the left of the hen-run shed, with some poached ground leading to a hand-gate and short passage between dwellings to a wall-stile adjacent to the tiny stone barn conversion 'Harry's Barn'.

21 Go left along the village road in the utterly delightful Maulds Meaburn. The village-name alludes to the feudal granting of the estate in 1174 by William de Veteriponte to his wife Maud, and Meaburn 'meadow by the stream' from a time when this land was in Scotland! You may take the early opportunity to inspect the rustic Lyvennet weir, feeding a long-retired millstream. The village is set about a generous meadow and you can wander by either upstream via the footbridges and mid-point road-bridge or stay with the road. Should you stay with the immediate road, passing through the narrows by Midtown Farm, subsequently take the open side road

River Lyvennet in Maulds Meaburn

footpath signed 'Crosby Ravensworth'. This leads, via a cattle-grid (composed of railway tracks) on the roadway and passing a white weather-boarded house, to the ornate gates of the ostentatious Victorian Flash House. Go through the adjacent hand-gate along the path to slip through a gated underpass into a meadow. Traverse to a stone squeeze-stile, walking on beside the Lyvennet before coming by a wall to cross a small bridge, spotting a charming bronze motif of a Greater Spotted Woodpecker on a post. Next, cross the stepped wall-stile, continuing beside the tree-lined river in the meadow to a red-painted metal hand-gate leading through the paddock beside the farmhouse of Low Row Farm to a red wooden hand-gate exiting onto the road. Go right, note the 'sign of our times' blue SAT NAV warning road-sign.

22 Cross the Monks Bridge, observing the confluence of Dalebanks Beck with the River Lyvennet - this river-name is genuinely Welsh and gained honorable mention in Arthurian legend. The cottage Monks Bridge has a Latin inscription above its door "Ingredere ut proficias" which in English reads "Enter in order to profit". Turn left to join the path passing St Lawrence's, the parish church of Crosby Ravensworth; of considerable architectural interest to church aficionados. On a more informal level you will enjoy the chatter of rooks in the mature trees that give the church shelter and perusing the circular road-side stone with interest. The path comes onto the next road past the Parish Archives and near left find refreshment in the Butchers Arms - Lyvennet Community Pub, pride of the Crosby Ravensworth locality. The pub-name refers to the Duke of Cumberland, who gained the less-than-flattering nickname through his ruthless handling of the retreating Highland army at the tail-end of the Jacobite Rebellion.

23 Go straight on, maintaining company with Dalebanks Beck on a minor road up the side valley leading by Low Dalebanks, a farmstead that has been attractively converted into three dwellings. Not obvious from the valley, but up to your left is an enclosure known as Ewe Close (with no public access); this is the site of an extensive Romano-British settlement. Through the site ghosts the Roman road from Low Borrow Bridge to Kirkby Thore, passing on invisibly through the Lyvennet valley. The tarmac road ends at High Dalebanks, from where a green bridle-track continues, ascending via a sequence of gates to the farming hamlet of Oddendale. This peaceful little haven derives its name from the feminine-name Odeline, hence we have just ascended her valley and charming it was too, don't you agree?

24 Coming through the gated farmyard and track, emerge from the shelter-belt crossing a cattle-grid with a road which bears right, so uniting with Alfred Wainwright's perennially popular Coast to Coast Walk. Before the top of the rise, bear off the road left with an open track which leads alongside the fence and bank screening Hardendale Quarry, largely filled with a lake, a giant extraction linked to Shap limeworks. The walk is ushered off right by facing steps: in crossing the exit to the quarry, beware the occasional passage of some pretty hefty dumper trucks. Cross a fence-stile and step up through the limestone outcrop to contour across the hillside continuing in a north-westerly direction. You can make a detour from the popular trail by veering up under the ascending line of limestone outcrops onto the twin-cairned top of Hardendale Nab (372m/1220ft), for its extra special all-round view; slant half-right to find an easy way down onto the open road where a line of telegraph poles cross. Otherwise stick with the Coast to Coast Walk and in due course cross the open road below The Nab House enclosure to reach a gate. Continue with some large pink granite erratic boulders littering the thorn scrub slope, often grazed by ponies. Coming under a wall, contour beside a fence to reach a kissing-gate and footbridge crossing the M6 motorway.

25 Once across, angle half-right traversing the pasture to a wall-stile. Continue on the same line across the next pasture to a wall-stile beside a gate and, fording a tiny stream, advance to a hand-gate where you enter a green lane. Follow the lane passing shacks, winding down to cross the West Coast mainline, perhaps witnessing a Virgin Trains' Pendolina in 'full flight'. The route weaves through the housing estate by Moss Grove to reach the A6, Shap's main street, opposite the King's Arms.

26 The A6 is an ancient north/south corridor of human travel through the village. Turn right and follow the footway passing the Memorial Park brimming with a grand mix of recreational facilities and then old Market Hall Heritage Centre, home of Shap Local History Society. The Shap Outdoor Swimming Pool is the highest outdoor heated pool in the Country! There are two asides worth considering. Short of the Abbey Coffee Shop ascend Jackson Lane to visit the parish church of Michael's. This just might this stand on a pagan site, perhaps associated with the village-name, which means 'heap of stones'.

Indeed, the village is renowned for its ancient stones, there is a two-mile long stone avenue to the west aligned with the massive freestanding Goggleby Stone - which you can also visit by turning left at the Fire Station, following a field-path by hand-gates and wall-stiles. This is part of a megalith complex with connected burial mounds. Passing the popular Shap Chippy, come to a junction, opposite the New Ing Lodge (a simply superb independent hostel).

Goggleby Stone, Shap

DAY FOUR

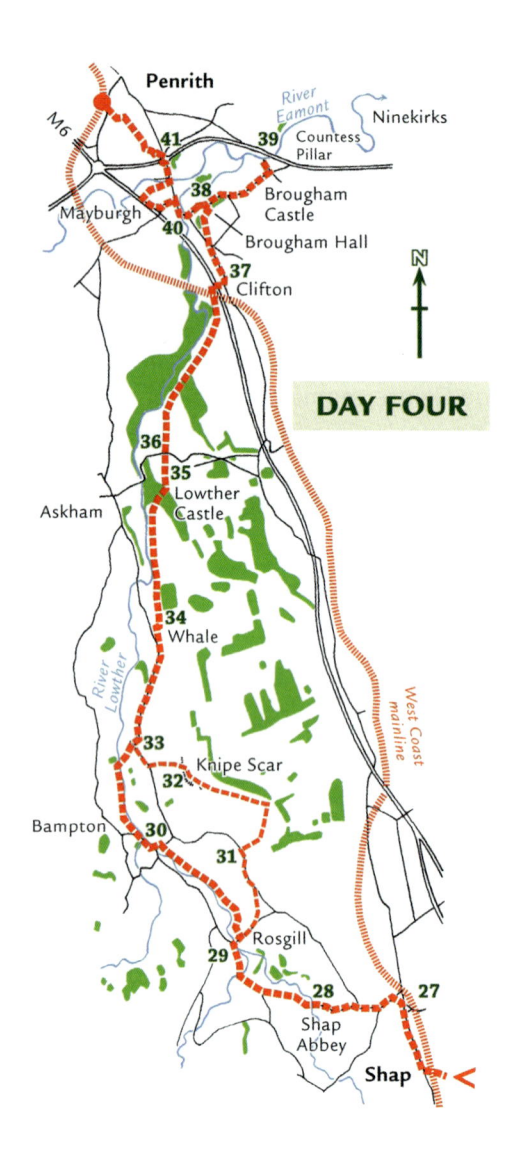

Penrith
M6
River Eamont
Ninekirks
Countess Pillar
41
39
38
Brougham Castle
Mayburgh
40
Brougham Hall
37
Clifton

N ↑

36
35
Lowther Castle
Askham

34
Whale

River Lowther

West Coast mainline

33
32
Knipe Scar
Bampton
30
31

29
Rosgill

28
27
Shap Abbey
Shap

32

DAY FOUR   Shap to Penrith
23km/14 miles   7½ hours

A rousing rising crescendo. This final leg takes fullest pleasure from the Lowther valley, interspersed with places of refreshment, at Bampton Grange, Lowther Castle and Brougham Hall.

27 Our next intermediate destination is Shap Abbey a mile distant, reached by following the road to the left. You can keep to the road all the way, though there is a field-path option immediately adjacent joined at the double-gate soon after leaving the village where two footpaths are signed into a field. Keep left, coming up to a wall-stile tight by the road at the wall-junction. Keep beside the wall exiting via a gate onto the Rosgill road, but go straight on, via the facing wall-stile behind the brown 'Shap Abbey' sign. Continue close to the roadside wall, wary of a damp patch by a cattle trough, to reach a second wall-stile from where one steps down onto an open concrete roadway. You can follow this down or head straight

Shap Abbey

33

down the pasture, cross the roadway and pass by the bungalow to cross the stone bridge spanning the River Lowther, signed 'Shap Abbey pedestrians only', adjacent to the monument's free car park. Passing through a gate, the wall-side track leads to the farm-roadway. The tall tower of Shap Abbey stands graciously before you, where serenity and peace abides. In the custodianship of English Heritage a stroll about the ruins is time well spent (entry fee). The setting includes a farm, its hen run adding to the sense of timelessness in a rural idyll.

28 Step back towards the gate, veering up the bank to go through a hand-gate. Now contour on a trod above the steep bank overlooking the river, to enter the open pasture, contouring across the field to a gate. The path heads on, fording a gill to climb to the brow, running on with the wall close left. Ignore the gate in front of you. Continue with the wall and, where it ends, bear half-left to find a low stile across the line of an old boundary line ditch feature - in all probability associated with the monastic estate. Weave through the rushes to a stile beside a padlocked gate, stepping out onto an open road. Go right and at the left-hand bend bear right, passing through a hand-gate adjacent to a ruined farmstead with a crumpled Dutch barn. Head on down the paddock to a wall-stile and continue straight down the field to the left-hand side of the trees, slipping down the bank to a hand-gate to cross Parish Crag Bridge. This enchanting packhorse bridge sits on a bend of Swindale Beck, the setting deserves time out to absorb the shy beauty of the place. Follow on beside the fence next to Fairy Crag to a gated wall-stile, now beside a wall beneath Goodcroft to join its access track. Keep forward with the track, via a hand-gate and then field-gate onto the minor road. Turn right and cross Rosgill Bridge, studying the River Lowther up and down stream from its refuges. The river-name derives from 'lathering water'.

Parish Crag Bridge spanning Swindale Beck

29 You have a choice of routes from this point, either continue at valley level or if you have the time and energy sweep over the scarp crest of Knipe Scar, a truly magnificent viewpoint - not to be lightly dismissed!

VALLEY ROUTE via Bampton Grange

After 100m turn left, following the side road to Hegdale Farm - named from the bird-cherry tree, also known as hagberry. Where the road bends up into the farmyard, continue forward in the walled lane, passing a barn to enter a meadow at a gate. Keep with the wall-side track and go through another field-gate, continuing through the next meadow to a gill-spanning plank and gate connecting into a long meadow. Begin beside the river-side fence, latterly drifting over to the right-hand side of the field to cross facing wall-stiles (the second having a small gate) through a short walled lane below a barn. Traverse the next field to a hand-gate, continuing direct to the church. Step over a stone flag and, via a kissing-gate, go through the churchyard passing the chancel end of St Patrick's Church, with its Georgian features. This brings you to a metal hand-gate onto the street, opposite the Crown & Mitre Hotel in Bampton Grange.

30 Turn left crossing the Lowther bridge to veer right along the road signed to Bampton – which has a pub, the Mardale Arms, and a shop with a seasonally open café. After the next bridge, spanning Haweswater Beck, go through the kissing-gate on the right and traverse the small field to a hand-gate. Pursue a low bank to a wicket-gate, then on upon the riverbank, with evidence of active river erosion eating into the bank at one point. Arriving at a gated suspension bridge over the broad shallow river, stride over and follow on with the path over damp ground with some gorse on Knipe Common. The path gradually rises to come onto the open road opposite the old Knipe phone box.

HIGH-LEVEL ROUTE via Knipe Scar

Rosgill means 'horse-valley'. Ascend the village street, lined by a sequence of re-invigorated vernacular cottages. Turn left into a lane by The Lindens, where you invariably will be greeted by a diverse selection of chickens. A walled lane winds peacefully on, gradually gaining height to meet the Shap to Lowther valley road. This tends to be quite a busy little thoroughfare. Turn left. Notice the curious little obelisk up the field on the near brow right, this is known as Mary's Pillar, erected in 1854 by Thomas Castley of Thorn. The family has been rooted in the Rosgill locality since the Middle Ages and a descendant lives here still - one suspects the elevated spot has a lovely view over the Lowther valley, though there is no public access to it. Keep with the road until a side road branches right, quaintly signed 'Scarside'.

31 Follow this walled lane up past the charmingly rustic environs, the farmstead featured as a location in the cult film 'Withnail and I'. Follow on up the continuing green lane to a gate, from where an open track angles up left, skirting the gorse forest to reach a tall gate in the ridge-top wall. Do not go through. Instead turn left and follow the wall, shielded by the rank gorse and shelter-belt. These trees, beech and larch, deny you a glimpse of the Three Battalions, a trio of landscaped

Looking west across the Lowther valley from Knipe Scar

beech clumps, strikingly in view from points way north. The near tall wall is beautifully built of higgledy-piggledy limestone rock. As the ridge widens so the quad track trends away from the wall, you may even prefer to hold to the very edge for the very best views en route to the topmost point of Knipe Scar (342m/1122ft). Quite a modest height for such a stupendously impressive view. At your feet, notice a circular Ordnance Survey triangulation plate. There is almost a complete panorama: east to Cross Fell; south to the Howgill Fells and west the high skyline of the Far Eastern Fells, traversed by the High Street Roman road, with the field and woods of the delightful Lowther valley regaled below.

If you have Druidical leanings, you might be intrigued to find the stone circle in the limestone pavement close to the woodland bounding wall due east. Although, if the bracken is rank, you'll see nothing. In fact, even when the bracken has died back in winter, but for the solitary stake marking its site, you'd question its credentials! If you go hunting, make a point of returning to the summit to continue upon the Castles of Eden Walk. Knipe incidentally means 'projecting rock', though it is hard to suggest to which rock it might apply.

32 Walk on north coming quickly into a nick. Descend through this way and angle right finding a sheep trod above the gorse then, as this relents, the path turns down to join a clearer turf track. This has its moments of mud and brushes with gorse before it sweeps through a saturated hollow and advances to join an

open road. Turn right shortly and, passing an old milk churn stand, duly arriving at the Knipe phone box - it won't ring a bell as you've not been here before and there is no phone! But it passes for a local information centre which is 'smart'. This is the point where the HIGH-LEVEL ROUTE meets the VALLEY ROUTE.

33 Go through the adjacent road-gate following the continuing open road through the hollow – note the gushing spring resurgence to the left. Swinging up left via a further road-gate (invariably open), hold to the quiet road passing a couple of shippon barns, with a cottage in between. As the road levels watch for a footpath signed 'Whale' off to the right via a hand-gate. Drift down the long pasture field to a further hand-gate coming to a clapper-bridge over Whale Beck (below). Advance up the field to a hand-gate left of a cottage. This is Whale, a curious hamlet-name that owes its origins to the Norse 'hvall' meaning 'round hill'. Although, like Knipe, it's rather hard to suggest precisely where the implied hill-feature might be.

34 Turn right coming up to the triangular green. To avoid walking through the environs of Whale Farm and disturbing the hounds in their kennels, take the footpath signed 'Lowther Park' left above Denfold Cottage (with incorporated barn). Cross the wall step-stile and follow the confined passage to a further wall step-stile, stepping down into a pasture. The walk thereby neatly by-passes the farm buildings, which are over to your right. Once beyond, go through successive kissing-gates to enter a farm-track beside an open coppice woodland. Follow this track left emerging into pasture at a gate. Keep on as another track from Crookholme Bridge merges from the left. Coming close to the River Lowther once more, go through the next gate and march merrily along the track in harmony with the river, passing a gravel area where a gallery of perhaps two dozen beehives is often stationed. After the next gate wander on through a parkland landscape, the skyline up to your right rimmed with low limestone scars (crags). At the second gate/hand-gate enter woodland and keep with the main rising track which comes up to a cattle-grid and so runs on close to the outer mock battlement walls of the ornate Lowther Castle.

35 Some works have been effected to revive the fabric of this amazing fantasy castle. The visitor appeal of this remarkable place is understandable and you are encouraged to call by the shop or café, or take a tour of

Lowther Castle courtyard aspect

Jack's Yak

the magnificent landscaped gardens backing the obvious façade. You may access the tea-room in the castle courtyard by wandering on beside the walls beyond the gatehouse (no access), going through the gate and subsequent rough paddock to another gate joining the normal flow of visitors from the main car park. Otherwise the Castles of Eden Walk follows on the open track away from the gatehouse, but first glance down the handsome northerly vista avenue, a little over a mile long. The track forks, keep left down the curving avenue to cross the public road, which leads through the park from Hackthorpe to Askham. You might wish to see 'Jack's Yak', reputedly the oldest oak tree in Cumbria, which stands up the road to the right, its aged limb cradled.

36 Following on from the road with Duke Henry's Drive, watch to take the right-hand rising gravel track, at the fork where the Drive shapes to descend towards Low Gardens Bridge. Cross a cattle-grid, now with the fence close left, which leads through a passage where a beck flows through woodland on either side, noting the curious chapel-like pump-house to the right. Shortly a track merges from the right, continue to Buckholme Lodge passing through a hand-gate to exit Lowther Park. The track continues unenclosed through pasture via a stile/field-gate. At this point you can inspect two innominate standing stones (below): detour right, the footpath enters a farm-lane and the stones lie 100m from the galvanised gate. Otherwise, keep forward and the track soon enters a fenced lane, swinging left as it comes alongside the M6 motorway and passing under the elevated West Coast mainline 'fly-over'. The farm access track takes a right turn to follow suit by Clifton Hall Bridge, promptly arriving upon Clifton Hall Pele Tower, a striking edifice. You can enter the enclosure in the care of English Heritage, climb the steps and marvel at the magical interior. Read the interpretation panels and orbit the C15th manor house, which is a remnant of the far larger defended hall structure that seems to have begun life in about 1400 and which had a practical life of some four centuries. The most substantial defended hall was built by William Wybergh at a turbulent time of Border Reiving. In the early C19th the adjacent farmhouse became the preferred residence and most of the old hall was demolished, the masonry inevitably re-cycled into farm buildings. There is no

Clifton Hall pele tower

right-of-way through the farmyard beyond, so step back and skirt right from a metal kissing-gate under the tall wall. Round left at a stile, then by gates passing a horse paddock and go through a parking area up to the wall-stile onto the footway beside the A6 opposite Clifton parish church.

37 The village-sign leaves new visitors in no doubt about the community's place in history, this being the scene of the last land battle on English soil in 1745 at the tail-end of the Jacobite Rebellion, when Bonnie Prince Charlie's bedraggled retreating Highland army was routed by the Duke of Cumberland. If nothing else, it is a reminder of the arterial nature of the road down the centuries, reinforced by the not incidental passage of the adjacent M6 motorway. Clifton, which translates as "the farm at the top of a bank" has a top notch gastro-pub, the George and Dragon, but sadly for anyone in a hurry, this lies at the far end of the community! The parish church of St Cuthbert's, on the other hand, could not be any handier. A few minutes devoted to calmly looking at this medieval place of worship is time well spent. The walk now turns left following the footway downhill from the Old Rectory, passing the village sign and later a handsome bank-barn. At the Clifton Cross road junction, go at an angle to and through the 'door' in the wall, from where a footpath leads across the rising field to come alongside the top of a wooded

Brougham Hall

Brougham Castle

bank, skirting along the field margin. Rounding the field corner, as house gardens intervene, step over a fence-stile and follow a confined path alongside the gardens. Emerging, find a fence-stile left passing a garden gazebo at the corner of a garden to gain the road over a wall-stile. Bear left and right to pass the gatehouse of Brougham Hall.

38 Since the awful floods of December 2015, when Brougham Castle Bridge was damaged, no public access is now permitted. At that time many another bridge suffered cruelly, famously the upstream Pooley Bridge at the outflow of Ullswater, which was swept away. Hence in order to get up close and personal with Brougham Castle one has to do a there and back minor road foray from Brougham Hall.

Turn right, following the quiet country road to the Brougham cross-roads, where you go left. Attention should be given on the sheep pasture to the left containing the slight banks outlining the Roman fort Brocavum constructed in 72AD – the Roman name reflecting the British term for 'where broom grows', hence Brougham is pronounced 'broom'.

39 The concrete A66 bridge downstream is thought to rest upon the foundations of the Roman bridge on the main road north to Voreda (Plumpton) and Luguvalium (Carlisle). Beyond, the river heads east for a quiet union with the Eden, by a minor Roman road ford at Udford. Study both the great flow of water and the striking position of the castle. Upstream see the watersmeet, with the Lowther flowing in from the left.

However, you are obliged to backtrack to Brougham Hall to complete the journey to Penrith.

38 No one passing through the Brougham Hall courtyard entrance can evade the narrative plea to support the works to restore this Tudor pile. Each summer the Globe Theatre puts on a Shakespeare play on the turf staging within, a most atmospheric setting. A series of craft studios and specialist shops are contained within, plus the all-essential coffee shop. During the Victorian Age the name Brougham was synonymous with a single-horse drawn carriage – made fashionable by Henry Brougham, Lord Chancellor in 1830, who lived here. Until the arrival of the motor car, it was the vehicle of choice 'about town' for the well to do. So from the entrance door, head west taking a moment to admire the door knocker on the original front door, a facsimile of the famous dragon's head knocker on Durham Cathedral. This is one of four replicas made in 1927 to replace the C12th original, which is now locked away in the Cathedral treasury. Pass under the bridge, which was an access from the hall to the little parish church of St Wilfrid. Follow the road and use its old line by the lodge on a path to reach the A6 footway and bridge over the River Lowther.

40 See the Lowther Lodge left, a mini replica of the Castle. At the road junction go left, noting the South African memorial on the facing field corner. Given time, go through the kissing-gate to inspect King Arthur's Round Table: the name is fictitious, the monument is not. This is a ceremonial site some four thousand years old that begs far more questions than can be answered, though it must have been intertwined with Mayburgh. Continue with the footway to reach the Millenium Stone - installed as a unifying statement of the faiths of Eden - here bear down the side road signed to Southwaite Green Mill. Again, a kissing-gate invites access to inspect Mayburgh Henge, a great doughnut shaped ringwork with a solitary standing stone in its midst: once there was a circle of eight. The henge, a cathedral of its age, is composed of beckstone carried by pilgrims, probably the accumulation of many centuries. The road passes Southwaite Green cottages seeking a footpath signed right which leads through to the Bleach Green access drive. Follow the river downstream to the handsome Eamont Bridge, the one survivor from the cruel floods of December 2015 though it did need masonry repairs. There are two pubs in the village as further lure.

41 But, if time is pressing, cross the road at the traffic lights and the metal footbridge ascending Kemplay Bank. Cross the broad busy road near the top where KEEP CLEAR is painted on the road. Pass in front of the old toll bar bungalow to reach the pedestrian crossing using the lights on a very busy traffic roundabout junction. Follow the footway on round by the roundabout to enter the confined footpath leading to the suburban street Wetheriggs Lane. Keep forward, passing Penrith cricket club and Ullswater Community College after the next road junction from the right and, coming to the rear of the Sainsbury's car park, turn left

Penrith Castle

with Castle Hill Road. Veer right with the first cul-de-sac. Follow the path up a brief bank and cross an intervening road continuing by the fence-confined path into Castle Park. Keep straight on, rounding the pavilion following the tree avenue, with Penrith Castle close right. You might take the opportunity to inspect your final castle set in Castle Park. See the English Heritage information board before the steps through the moat. Even now the great new red sandstone walls retain a strong sense of how imposing the bastion was when entire, emphasised by a deep moat. Unlike the fortifications thrown up by Edward I in the 14th century, this castle emerged more piecemeal a century later. During the original construction of the Shap to Carlisle section of the West Coast mainline railway completed in 1846, many of its 1,000 horses used were stabled in the confines of the castle. Go through the arched gated entrance and over the busy road, coming directly upon the forecourt of Penrith West Coast Mainline railway station. Bon voyage!

Customising Your Castles of Eden Expedition

You might undertake this walk either as the complete four-day 42-mile expedition, or in two long weekend two-day rambles, walking Kirkby Stephen to Appleby (17 miles) and then Appleby to Penrith (25 miles).

Ordnance Survey Maps

Landranger maps 90 and 91

Outdoor Leisure maps 5 and 19

Tourist Information & Where to Stay advice

Kirkby Stephen – Upper Eden Visitor Centre, Market Square visit@uecp.org.uk   017683 71199

Appleby-in-Westmorland – Moot Hall, Boroughgate tic@applebytown.org.uk 017683 51177

Penrith – Old Robinson's School, Penrith & Eden Museum, Middlegate pen.tic@eden.gov.uk 01768 867466

Train & Bus Connections

The core focus of this station to station walk is the Settle-Carlisle Railway station at Kirkby Stephen, served by Northern Rail. The walk's objective is Penrith, from where you can board a Virgin Trains Pendolino/Voyager for your homeward connections. There is also a Stagecoach bus service 574 on a Tuesday between Kirkby Stephen – Appleby-Penrith and back, one bus each way. Further you might relish undertaking this walk using other bus links, such as the X5 Trans-Cumbria from Keswick, via the Penrith connection. Details on Cumbria CC website www.cumbria.gov.uk

Taxis

APPLEBY-IN-WESTMORLAND

Appleby Taxis Crosscroft Industrial Estate 017683 52382

MMK Appleby Taxis   Long Marton Road 017683 53106

JVR Taxis   Midtown Farmhouse, Long Marton   017683 52382

PENRITH

Abbey Taxis of Penrith   www.abbeytaxisofpenrith.co.uk 07789 023023

A1 Acclaim Taxis www.penrith-taxi.co.uk   01768 866842

Ace Taxis www.acetaxispenrith.co.uk   01768 890731

A Taxis 01768 863354

Eden Taxis www.edentaxispenrith.co.uk   01768 865 432

Penrith Taxis   01768 899298

Town Taxis www.towntaxispenrith.com 01768 868268

KIRKBY STEPHEN

Alan Middleton 07930 856778

BD Taxis Soulby 017683 71682

Prima Taxis   017683 72557

Steady Eddies   017683 72036